LISTENING TO GOD

10 STUDIES FOR INDIVIDUALS OR GROUPS

LifeGuide®
BIBLE STUDIES

CAROLYN NYSTROM

IVP Connect
An imprint of InterVarsity Press
Downers Grove, Illinois

With thanks to my dear friends Jan, Shirley, Kathy, Linda, Beverley, Agnes, Jude and Sherri, who helped me try out this study.

InterVarsity Press
P.O. Box 1400, Downers Grove, IL 60515-1426
www.ivpress.com
email@ivpress.com

InterVarsity Press® is the book-publishing division of InterVarsity Christian Fellowship/USA®, a movement of students and faculty active on campus at hundreds of universities, colleges and schools of nursing in the United States of America, and a member movement of the International Fellowship of Evangelical Students. For information about local and regional activities, write Public Relations Dept., InterVarsity Christian Fellowship/USA, 6400 Schroeder Rd., P.O. Box 7895, Madison, WI 53707-7895, or visit the IVCF website at www.intervarsity.org.

LifeGuide® is a registered trademark of InterVarsity Christian Fellowship

All Scripture quotations, unless otherwise indicated, are taken from THE HOLY BIBLE, NEW INTERNATIONAL VERSION®, NIV® Copyright © 1973, 1978, 1984, 2011 by Biblica, Inc.™ Used by permission. All rights reserved worldwide.

While any stories in this book are true, some names and identifying information may have been changed to protect the privacy of the individuals involved.

Design: Cindy Kiple
Images: © Dirk Wustenhagen / Trevillion Images

ISBN 978-0-8308-3110-4 (print)
ISBN 978-0-8308-6428-7 (digital)

Printed in the United States of America ∞

P	20	19	18	17	16	15	14	13	12	11	10	9	8	7	6	5	4	3	2
Y	33	32	31	30	29	28	27	26	25	24	23	22	21	20	19	18	17		

Contents

Getting the Most Out of *Listening to God*

How does a person listen to God?

For some Christians, listening to God is a constant inner tuning to nudges from the Spirit as we go about our day: eat this, say that, read this, pray—always pray. Others seem to hear God mostly through Scripture. They read the Scripture and listen to scholars of the Scripture to better understand its meaning and context. And they try to live it out to the best of their understanding and ability. They pray too, though perhaps not with an intent of listening for a personal message from God. I confess that I lean more toward the second category of listeners than the first, though I've had my experiences with nudges apparently from God. And I have dear friends who are accomplished at that kind of listening.

How did the people of Scripture listen to God?

For some it seemed no effort at all. Adam and Eve walked in the garden God had made for them and talked with him, and he with them. Something went wrong after that, and we rarely see a physical appearance of God thereafter—until Jesus himself arrives: God in human form. Meanwhile, Hagar, in deep distress, hears words of courage from "the angel of the LORD" (Genesis 16:7). Or was this being actually God? Hagar named him "the God who sees me" (Genesis 16:13). Moses also had a verbal encounter with God, but God protected Moses from a personal sighting saying, "I will put you in a cleft in the rock and cover you with my hand" (Exodus 33:22). God spoke to many other biblical characters: Elijah, Solomon and Ezekiel, and of course to many humans during the time Jesus walked on earth. But afterward—long afterward—Jesus spoke again to John.

People of our era are not responsible for creating Holy Scripture, as were many of these God listeners. But we have those Scriptures by which God speaks to us. What can we learn from them about the spiritual discipline of listening to God?

Suggestions for Individual Study

1. As you begin each study, pray that God will speak to you through his Word.

2. Read the introduction to the study and respond to the personal reflection question or exercise. This is designed to help you focus on God and on the theme of the study.

3. Each study deals with a particular passage so that you can delve into the author's meaning in that context. Read and reread the passage to be studied. The questions are written using the language of the New International Version, so you may wish to use that version of the Bible. The New Revised Standard Version is also recommended.

4. This is an inductive Bible study, designed to help you discover for yourself what Scripture is saying. The study includes three types of questions. Observation questions ask about the basic facts: who, what, when, where and how. Interpretation questions delve into the meaning of the passage. Application questions help you discover the implications of the text for growing in Christ. These three keys unlock the treasures of Scripture.

Write your answers to the questions in the spaces provided or in a personal journal. Writing can bring clarity and deeper understanding of yourself and of God's Word.

5. It might be good to have a Bible dictionary handy. Use it to look up any unfamiliar words, names or places.

6. Use the prayer suggestion to guide you in thanking God for what you have learned and to pray about the applications that have come to mind.

7. You may want to go on to the suggestion under "Now or Later," or you may want to use that idea for your next study.

Suggestions for Members of a Group Study

1. Come to the study prepared. Follow the suggestions for individual study mentioned above. You will find that careful preparation will greatly enrich your time spent in group discussion.

2. Be willing to participate in the discussion. The leader of your group will not be lecturing. Instead, he or she will be encouraging the members of the group to discuss what they have learned. The leader will be asking the questions that are found in this guide.

3. Stick to the topic being discussed. Your answers should be based on the verses that are the focus of the discussion and not on outside authorities such as commentaries or speakers. These studies focus on a particular passage of Scripture. Only rarely should you refer to other portions of the Bible. This allows for everyone to participate in in-depth study on equal ground.

4. Be sensitive to the other members of the group. Listen attentively when they describe what they have learned. You may be surprised by their insights! Each question assumes a variety of answers. Many questions do not have "right" answers, particularly questions that aim at meaning or application. Instead the questions push us to explore the passage more thoroughly.

When possible, link what you say to the comments of others. Also, be affirming whenever you can. This will encourage some of the more hesitant members of the group to participate.

5. Be careful not to dominate the discussion. We are sometimes so eager to express our thoughts that we leave too little opportunity for others to respond. By all means participate! But allow others to also.

6. Expect God to teach you through the passage being discussed and through the other members of the group. Pray that you will have an enjoyable and profitable time together, but also that as a result of the study you will find ways that you can take action individually and/or as a group.

7. Remember that anything said in the group is considered confidential and should not be discussed outside the group unless specific permission is given to do so.

8. If you are the group leader, you will find additional suggestions at the back of the guide.

1

The God Who Speaks

Genesis 1–3

The God of creation is a God who communicates. If we are to learn to listen to God, we must understand something of his voice and the character of God revealed in that voice. Rarely in Scripture do we find so many times the phrase "God said" as in the first three chapters of Genesis. There, in the opening words of Scripture, God begins to reveal his character—through his voice.

GROUP DISCUSSION. When you try to imagine "the voice of God," what do you hear, see, think, imagine?

PERSONAL REFLECTION. God followers have many different ideas about how and under what circumstances God speaks or has spoken. List several concepts you currently believe about God speaking.

"In the beginning God . . ." constitutes the opening phrase of the Bible in almost any language. And within a few lines the reader hears the voice of God over and over. *Read Genesis 1–3*. Note or mark each spot where you find the words *God said*.

---

1. What happened when "God said . . ."?

2. Take another visual trip through these chapters and mark other actions of God, finding such phrases as: God called, God saw, God made, God set, God created, God found, God breathed. As you encounter each of these phrases, how would you describe the character of God who said and did this or that?

---

3. What signs of order do you find in the creation acts of Genesis 1?

---

4. Look again at Genesis 1:26-30. What is unique about God's creation of humans: How are humans similar and how are they different from his other creations?

---

5. Focus particularly on Genesis 1:27. What can you discern from the term "image of God" as it relates to a spiritually healthy view of yourself?

---

6. How might the "image of God" affect the way you relate to people you know and don't know?

7. Genesis 2 is a retelling of creation, but this time with a different focus. What similarities and differences do you find in these two chapters?

What special care did God give to humans?

8. Mentally review the events of Genesis 3. What are some ways that the first humans were like God in ability and in character?

How were they different from God?

9. What hints of hope do you find in such a dark, cosmic event?

10. "In Adam's Fall, We sinned all," *The New England Primer* (for children) said in 1777. What truths and what difficulties do you find in that statement?

11. If you could be an invisible bystander in any scene from Genesis 1:1–3:24, which would you choose and why?

12. Why might you want to learn to listen to God as he reveals himself in these first three chapters of the Bible?

Thank God for something that you saw in the first three chapters of Genesis.

Now or Later

Using your best dramatic voice to reflect the various emotions in the text, read aloud Genesis 1–3. After, focus on one sentence that uses the words God said. Repeat it several times. Meditate on its implications

- in humans relating to each other
- on revealing the character of God
- on your own place in God's creation
- on your value of other portions of his creation
- on your relationship with a God who speaks with such power

Turn your meditation to prayer as you respond to God.

2

Listening to the God Who Hears

Genesis 16:1-15; 18:1-33

Eons have passed since our last study. The first man and first woman and their descendants have populated the earth. People groups and then nations formed. Language, distance, geography and culture divided these people. So they warred against each other. Few knew or followed the God of creation. God intervened—again—this time to appoint a people group who would continue to know and follow him. God started with one man, Abraham, and his wife, Sarah. Oddly (for a God who created and ruled the universe), God began by listening to these beings he had made.

GROUP DISCUSSION. Describe one situation when you felt you were heard.

PERSONAL REFLECTION. What does being heard do for your relationship with the person who listened to you?

In these texts you will find an almighty, all-knowing, all-powerful God who stoops to listen. *Read Genesis 16:1-15.* Note or mark each set of quotation marks.

1. What details reveal the various motives and emotions of the characters in verses 1-6?

Who do you most empathize with and why?

---

2. Focus on the conversation between Hagar and the angel of the Lord in verses 7-15. How did the angel of the Lord help Hagar to speak her heart?

---

3. What did the angel of the Lord reveal to Hagar?

If you had been Hagar, would you have wanted to know all this? Why or why not?

---

4. Look again Hagar's words in verse 13, "You are the God who sees me." What does this suggest about Hagar's understanding of God's care for her?

Read Genesis 18.

---

5. What are some ways that Abraham showed hospitality to his guests?

---

6. In view of the whole story, why do you think Sarah laughed (v. 12)?

---

7. The text identifies one of Abraham's three visitors as "the LORD." As you listen in to the conversation beginning at verse 16 between Abraham and his visitor, what appears to be the relationship between Abraham and "the LORD"?

---

8. What do you learn of the character of Abraham?

What did Abraham learn about the character of the Lord from this conversation?

9. In what ways was Abraham a richer man because of his time with the Lord?

---

10. Of what value to you is it that God hears your prayers even if he does not give all that you ask?

Pray, beginning with the words of Hagar, "You are the God who sees me." Then open your heart to the Lord who sees and listens to you.

Now or Later

Take an outdoor walk. Listen to the sound of God-created things: the rustle of leaves in the wind, the chirp of a bird, the crunch of grass beneath your feet, the scurry of a squirrel, the creak of a large tree bending ever so slightly in the wind, the rhythmic lapping of tidal water, the whisper of sand adjusting beneath your feet, the laughter of a child, your own breath. Add your own praise in song or prayer to the God who hears.

3

Listening to the God of Covenant

Exodus 33:7–34:14

Another seven hundred years or so have passed since our last study. The people of God are now organized into twelve tribes. They've spent a few hundred years in Egypt, first as honored guests as Joseph's relatives and later as slaves (possibly doing the manual labor of building the pyramids). They still worshiped Abraham's God and identified themselves as Hebrews. But they were in danger of becoming assimilated into the Egyptian culture and religion. God intervened again. This time God appointed Moses as their leader, who marched them out of Egypt. At God's command, the Red Sea closed in and drowned the pursuing Egyptians. Then God began the work of reeducating his people. He gave them (through Moses listening to God on a mountain top) the Ten Commandments, written on stone, beginning with "You shall have no other gods"—which the people broke by molding a gold calf and trying to worship it even before Moses got down from the mountain. Perhaps symbolizing an already-shattered relationship, Moses shattered against the rocks these "tablets of stone inscribed by the finger of God" (Exodus 31:18).

But God still wanted these people as his own. So he laid out a covenant with them to define that relationship.

GROUP DISCUSSION. What kinds of covenants do you see today?

PERSONAL REFLECTION. If God were to describe his covenant with you (how you and he relate to each other), what do you think he would say?

In this study you will find God beginning to carve a relationship with a people group he would call his own. *Read Exodus 33:7-11.*

1. What do you see here suggesting that what took place in the tent of meeting was no ordinary conversation?

2. Focus particularly on the first sentence of verse 11. What does this suggest about the relationship between God and Moses?

Read Exodus 33:12–34:14.

3. Have two people in your group read this passage aloud as a dialogue between Moses and God. Appoint a third person as narrator to read any sections not enclosed in quotation marks. What is the emotional impact of having heard this conversation between God and Moses?

4. Keeping in mind the covenant relationship being established between God and his people, what did God require of Moses?

5. What will God do and be for his people?

What did Moses ask of God?

---

6. What can you know of the character of God by hearing his conversation with Moses?

---

7. If you could have your own ideal relationship with God, what would that look like?

---

8. The word *name* appears five times in this text (Exodus 33:12, 17, 19; 34:5, 14). Reread each sentence where the word *name* appears. What seems important about each statement?

9. What difference does it make to you that God knows your name, and you know his?

---

10. Exodus 33:18-23 provides an illustration of the relationship between God and humans—even humans who are loved and chosen by God. What do you notice there about how God does and doesn't connect with his covenant people?

---

11. After God created a fresh copy of his commandments written in stone, God provided Moses with a fresh description of his character (Exodus 34:6-7). Would you have found this confronting or reassuring? Why?

---

12. Look at Exodus 34:10-14. What do you think God meant when he named himself "Jealous" in verse 14?

13. In view of the way God has identified himself to Moses in Exodus 34:4-6, why do you think Moses responded as he did in verses 8-9?

---

14. Would you do the same in your own setting? Why or why not?

Pray for someone you know who is not as close to God as you wish.

Now or Later

The dialogue between Moses and God in Exodus 33 provides an example for our own prayers. Pray a paraphrase of Moses' prayer drawn from verses 12-13. Insert your current greatest challenge in the space. Then continue to pray and meditate on that subject as you place yourself within the covenant care of God. Draw encouragement from God's response to Moses. He provides the same for us.

4

Listening to God When All Is Lost

1 Kings 19:1-21; 2 Kings 2:1-13

Almost 350 years have passed since Moses led the people of God out of Egypt into the desert toward the Promised Land, which would include (geographically) something like today's nation of Israel.

But the land was already inhabited by broadly scattered, frequently warring tribal groups clumped under the general title of Canaanites. The Hebrews also were divided into tribes based on which of Jacob's twelve sons from which they were descended. Through many years of war with the Canaanites, the Israelites settled into the land and divided it geographically among their own twelve tribes, each ruled by local judges (hence the Old Testament book of Judges). In about 1000 BC, these tribes united under King David and within a couple of generations divided into two clusters forming a northern kingdom and a southern kingdom. In general the southern kingdom comprised land occupied by the tribes of Judah and Benjamin, and these people continued to follow God. But the territory to the north, named after the rest of Jacob's sons, mostly assimilated into the Canaanite religions and culture. In the mid-800s BC, God sent his prophet Elijah to this northern kingdom with the difficult task of drawing these now near pagans back to the true God, who had covenanted with his people through Moses.

GROUP DISCUSSION. If you had been in Elijah's sandals with this task before you, what do you think you would have wanted from God?

PERSONAL REFLECTION. When you are faced with a near-impossible task, what are you likely to think of God?

By 850 BC the northern kingdom has been governed by King Ahab and his wife, Jezebel, for nearly two decades. Several times Elijah has confronted this ruling couple, most recently resulting in a massive slaughter of prophets of the Canaanite god Baal, with the consequence that Elijah now has a price on his head. You'll find the details in 1 Kings 17–18.

Today's reading will show a servant of God in despair, and a God who sees a larger picture. *Read 1 Kings 19:1-14.*

---

1. What reasons did Elijah have to be afraid?

What steps did Elijah take to save himself from Jezebel?

---

2. What notes of desperation do you find in Elijah's prayer of verse 4?

---

3. What are some ways God showed kindness to Elijah during his broom bush retreat?

4. When have you wished that you could meet God under a broom bush?

---

5. "The journey is too much for you," the angel said in verse 7. How might this have helped Elijah prepare for his two hundred-mile journey south to Horeb? (Consider physical, emotional, spiritual preparation.)

---

6. Have two group members read verses 9-14 as a dialogue between God and Elijah, using a narrator for the descriptive parts. How might various natural events help Elijah to know God?

---

7. Notice Elijah's words in verses 10 and 14, as he twice answers God's question, "What are you doing here?" What does Elijah's answer suggest to you about his nature and needs?

Read 1 Kings 19:15-21.

---

8. How might you have felt at God's first words, "Go back"?

As Elijah heard the rest of God's message (vv. 15-18), what encouragement would he find?

9. What evidence do you find in verses 19-21 that Elisha could become a capable successor to Elijah?

Read 2 Kings 2:1-13.

---

10. This event probably took place several years later, with Elijah discipling Elisha in the intervening time. Why do you think Elisha insisted on staying with Elijah?

---

11. What do you gain from this final scene of Elijah's story?

What do you wonder about?

Bring to God your greatest discouragements. Imagine yourself under a broom bush in the desert as you share with your Lord your hurt and your fear. Begin to trust his continuing presence. Acknowledge your dependence on him. Prepare to notice blessings of baked bread and jars of water that he supplies. If this is not true of you, pray for someone who seems similarly burdened.

Now or Later

What are some of your largest responsibilities? Begin to plan for an "Elisha" who you can mentor to share this load.

5

Listening as Worship

Ecclesiastes 5:1-7

What is this book—Ecclesiastes? Who wrote it? Why? When? For many books of the Bible, these questions sprout obvious answers. The author identifies himself as well as the time, place and purpose at the outset. For example: "Paul, an apostle of Christ Jesus by the will of God, to God's holy people in Ephesus" (Ephesians 1:1). Some leave a note of identity near the end of the book or letter. In other biblical books, the events recorded leave hints of time and place, and therefore author. But some books defy authorial identity. The book of Ecclesiastes is one of these.

True, at the outset we read, "The words of the Teacher, son of David, king in Jerusalem" (Ecclesiastes 1:1). These words point to Solomon, the son of David and Bathsheba born as a comfort to these parents after the death of their first son (2 Samuel 12:22-25). Solomon, known for his wisdom, ruled in Israel from about 971–931 BC. He was the last Hebrew king to rule a united kingdom. Elijah, with his ministry to the northern kingdom, would not come for another hundred years. Solomon was known for his wisdom; he also collected wise sayings and writings of others. So, did Solomon write the wisdom collection that we call Ecclesiastes? Or does "son of David" mean descendant of David, that is, many generations later? Or is this book a collection of wise saying from Solomon's era and therefore influenced by Solomon? Or did an unknown writer a few hundred years later create a wisdom book told in the first person as if the words came from the mouth of the great King Solomon? Thorough and godly scholars hold each of these positions (and others) as they attempt to answer: Who wrote the book of Ecclesiastes?

As we explore what the Bible says about the general subject of "listening to God," the author of Ecclesiastes contributes wise counsel and caution.

GROUP DISCUSSION. What aspects of worship do you value and why?

PERSONAL REFLECTION. When you put the words "listening" and "worship" together, what experiences, thoughts, worries and questions come to your mind?

"Worship is a verb," Robert Webber said in his 1985 book by the same title. It seems an ancient leader of worship agreed. *Read Ecclesiastes 5:1-7.*

1. What are some of the dos and don'ts of this passage?

2. What do these cautions about worship hint about the character of God?

3. What do you think the wisdom writer means when he says, "Guard your steps when you go to the house of God. Go near to listen" (v. 1)?

4. What are some ways you might guard your own preparation and presence in worship?

---

5. It seems there is a difference between listening and silence. How might either or both lead to worship?

---

6. Regarding vows (vv. 4-6), South African pastor and theologian Michael Eaton wrote, "The *vow* in ancient Israel was a promise to God, which might be part of a prayer of blessing (Num. 21:2) or a spontaneous expression of gratitude (Jon. 2:9). It might take the form of a promise of allegiance (Gen. 28:20-22), a free-will offering (Lev. 22:18), or the dedication of a child."* What kinds of vows or promises might show up in your own worship with other believers?

---

7. Verse 6 says, "Do not let your mouth lead you into sin." What kinds of sins might the author be thinking of?

---

*Michael Eaton, *Ecclesiastes*, Tyndale Old Testament Commentaries (Downers Grove, IL: IVP Academic, 2009), 114.

8. The writer of Ecclesiastes (a wordsmith and thinker by trade) proclaims in verse 7: "Much dreaming and many words are meaningless." What meaning would you give to that statement?

---

9. "Therefore fear God" marks the closing line of this ancient meditation (v. 7). Describe a time when you experienced something like fear or awe of God.

---

10. Reread aloud Ecclesiastes 5:1-7. What is one way that you would like to put some phrase or sentence of this text to work?

Spend five minutes in silent prayer, allowing your thoughts to express your worship, hopes, confessions and thanks to God. Use some of that time to listen to God. What might he be revealing about himself to you? At the end of this time whisper, "Amen."

Now or Later

Find an alone spot, preferably outdoors, and read aloud Psalm 148. Notice the many forms of nonverbal praise around you. Add your own silent worship to this praise of the God who made you, placed you in this setting and called you his own. When you are ready, give words or song to your worship.

6

Responsibility of a God Listener

The prophet Ezekiel speaks God's words from a harsh setting. The year is 587 BC. A decade prior, the people of God had been forced to march away from their homeland with its capital city of Jerusalem and the beautiful temple built by King Solomon nearly four hundred years earlier. Their evacuation took them to Babylon, a four month trip of nearly five hundred miles covered mostly on foot. Hostile forces marched them away from the land, people and temple that signified to them their God-given place in his universe.

GROUP DISCUSSION. What do you think would be hard about keeping the faith alive in Ezekiel's setting?

PERSONAL REFLECTION. What circumstances in your own setting make faith difficult for you or for people you know?

God continued to speak in the difficult setting of Babylonian captivity. Ezekiel continued to listen. *Read Ezekiel 33.*

1. Why might the Hebrews in this time and place need a spiritual watchman?

_____

2. What responsibilities and what protections are described for the watchman?

_____

3. Focus on verse 29. What seems to be the point of Ezekiel's task as a watchman?

_____

4. Reread verse 11. What can you see of God's heart in these words?

_____

5. Notice the message received in verse 21. If you were a Hebrew in Babylon hearing this news, what do you think you would do next?

How do you think this news would affect the work of Ezekiel, the God listener?

_____

6. What guidance might the Jews in Babylon receive from Ezekiel's words of warning (vv. 23-29)?

_____

7. In your own setting, who has functioned as a spiritual watcher for you?

How might you serve as a spiritual watcher for someone?

---

8. How might Ezekiel's experience as a God listener guide your own response to God's watchers?

---

9. Focus on verses 30-33. What might be difficult about the spiritual watcher's task (ancient or contemporary) in this setting?

---

10. As you reflect on your own experiences of giving and receiving good spiritual guidance, when might you thank God because "a prophet has been among" you (v. 33)?

Thank God for a particular person who has been a spiritual watcher for you. Then, if possible, send that person a message expressing your thanks.

Now or Later

God speaks to his people today primarily through Scripture. If you are a God listener, consider who might benefit from your relationship with God and your growing understanding of his Word. How and to whom might you best convey that important information?

7

Listening to Understand

Luke 24:13-53

Nearly six hundred years have passed since the prophet Ezekiel in our last study. During that time, the Babylonian culture declined after nearly a thousand years of influence. Rome, with its myth-like beginning of twins Romulus and Remus in the 700s BC, had become the world's governmental giant by Luke's era. Its empire totally surrounded the Mediterranean Sea, eventually claiming most of the known world and extending northward into much of what is now Europe.

Within this historical context we witness the birth, life, death and resurrection of Jesus.

GROUP DISCUSSION. When you are talking with someone, what helps you feel that you are being heard?

PERSONAL REFLECTION. If you had been able to accompany Jesus on the Emmaus Road, what do you think you would need to hear?

Today you get to take a seven-mile walk to Emmaus and talk with the risen Christ. *Read Luke 24:13-53.*

1. What are the circumstances behind this story that make this a good opportunity to listen to Jesus and understand him?

2. Why might you feel sympathetic toward these two disciples?

3. Pretend for a moment that you are a first-century traveler listening to the conversation of verses 13-29. What would interest you?

4. Focus on verses 30-35: "Then their eyes were opened" (v. 31). What do you think the two disciples saw in that moment of spiritual insight?

5. Consider the two who had this experience with Jesus and then tried to share it with the others (v. 35). What would you find difficult to talk about?

What would you try to emphasize?

6. In verses 36-49 Jesus interrupts the disciples' gathering. What do you find important about the details of this visit?

7. What do you think happened when "he opened their minds so they could understand the Scriptures" (v. 45)?

_____

8. What do you see when you picture the scenes in verses 36-53?

_____

9. What would you have gained (and lost) by being there?

_____

10. If you could have a conversation with one of the disciples who experienced all this, what would you ask?

Thank God for one of the events in this text.

Now or Later

Christ no longer walks bodily with us, but his Spirit remains within his people. Take time in the next week for a God walk. Consciously use that time to think and pray, and to reflect on your relationship with the ever-living Christ.

8

Holy Help in Listening

John (writer of the Gospel of John) and Luke (of our previous study) were contemporaries. Both lived during the lifetime of Jesus and were a part of establishing the early church. John takes a more theological approach to recounting the life and teachings of Jesus. In chapter 14 of John's Gospel, we see a beginning theology of the Holy Spirit, always present but shadowed in the Old Testament (as in Genesis 1:2 and Ezekiel 2:2) but now more clearly defined as a special gift: God present with and within his people after the earthly life of Jesus.

GROUP DISCUSSION. What are some of your wonderings about the Holy Spirit?

PERSONAL REFLECTION. Give thanks to God for the presence of his Spirit. Ask the Holy Spirit to help you better appreciate the text before you.

John was one of the three disciples closest to Jesus. Enjoy Jesus' loving encouragement to his closest friends. *Read John 14:5-31.*

1. Thomas, Philip and Judas each had a question for Jesus. What are the questions they ask?

What does each question suggest about their concerns as they talked together?

---

2. Focus on the dialogue between Jesus and Thomas in verses 5-7. What comfort might Thomas have found in Jesus' answer to his question?

Why might some be offended by Jesus' answer to Thomas?

---

3. What frustration do you sense in Philip as he says the words of verse 8?

---

4. In verses 9-21, Jesus gives a thorough reply to Philip's complaint. If you were in Philip's sandals, what would you find encouraging here?

---

5. What would you find scary or confusing in these same verses?

6. Focus on the question from Judas in verse 22. What worry do you sense in his question?

7. What do you find in Jesus' response (vv. 23-31) that would likely encourage Judas and the other remaining disciples?

8. Given your own current setting, what encouragement do you find in Jesus' words to Judas?

9. Review again each sentence of John 14:5-31. Using the information in this text, make as many true statements as you can about God as Trinity (three persons composing one God).

10. Notice the final words of this scene: "Come now; let us leave." Jesus and the disciples were departing for the Garden of Gethsemane. As you leave your own place of study, what concept or phrase from this text do you want to take with you as enter your next event?

Select one sentence from this passage that seems to have your name on it today. Make that a focus of prayer.

Now or Later

Spend time meditating on the presence of the Holy Spirit within you as described in John 14:17. Then throughout the day, allow God's Spirit to draw you to prayer. The following hymn, "Spirit of God, Descend Upon My Heart," written by George Croly in 1854, may further guide your worship.

Spirit of God, descend upon my heart;
wean it from earth, through all its pulses move;
stoop to my weakness, might as thou art,
and make me love thee as I ought to love.

Teach me to love thee as thine angels love,
one holy passion filling all my frame;
the baptism of the heaven-descended Dove,
my heart an alter, and thy love the flame.*

---

*For all five stanzas of "Spirit of God, Descend Upon My Heart" see www .hymnsite.com/lyrics/umh500.sht.

9

Listening as Self-Discipline

James 1:19-27

Who wrote the biblical book of James, when and why? Since James was a common name of the first century, and the book itself does little to reveal its human author, scholars have enjoyed theorizing on the subject. This speculation also extends to the book's timeframe. Was it as early AD 45, shortly after Christ's death? Or was it well into the second century, as part of the church era? Partly due to James's emphasis on Christian action rather than Christian belief, Martin Luther (1483–1546) termed the book "a right strawy Epistle" in the New Testament of 1522. So rather than poke at various background possibilities, we look instead at the book's teaching on the subject of listening to God.

Hearing is one thing; listening is quite another. Hearing is a matter of sound waves striking the eardrum and causing a vibration that the brain then interprets and gives meaning. Listening is hearing and much more. It has to do with practiced familiarity. One person might hear a high, rather scratchy noise from a violin. A violinist might hear a high C that's a trifle flat and in need of vibrato, with a little more ease on the bow. Learning to listen makes the difference.

GROUP DISCUSSION. What settings have caused you to listen with joy or delight? When do you listen with a measure of caution or anxiety?

PERSONAL REFLECTION. On a scale of one to ten, evaluate yourself as a listener. Ten means that you regularly listen to someone else with your whole being, asking appropriate questions and thinking carefully of the feelings, motives and implications behind what you hear. One means that when someone else is talking, you are thinking mostly of yourself with some similar experience or of what you might say next in the conversation.

We are privileged to read Scripture with our modern perspective, but also vicariously with the ears of the early church. Use both perspectives here. *Read James 1:19-27.*

---

1. Suppose you were an early Christian somewhere in the far reaches of the Roman Empire and this letter comes to your church. Your church leader reads it aloud at your Sunday gathering. What would you find helpful?

What would you find challenging?

What would you want to know more about?

---

2. What's hard about listening?

3. According to this text, what is the difference between hearing and listening?

4. Analyze verses 19-21. What are we to do and not to do? Why?

5. The section beginning with verse 22 instructs us, "Do not merely listen to the word, and so deceive yourselves." Why might listening to God's Word become a form of self-deception (use vv. 22-25)?

6. Focus on verse 25. Mentally walk yourself through your most recent participation in a worship service. (Feel free to reread your church bulletin, if available.) What could you do that would continue the worship you began there?

7. What are some practical steps you could take to continue the work begun in that particular worship service?

8. What might be difficult about practicing the kind of religion described in verses 26-27?

---

9. What listening practices would help a Christian hoping to do the work of verse 26-27?

---

10. Identify and share one area or relationship where you would like to better practice the self-discipline of listening described in this text.

Begin your prayer with a time of listening silence. Ask God to bring to your mind a relationship that might benefit by better listening on your part. Then pray for that person or situation inviting God's intervention.

Now or Later

Follow up on your listening prayer by scheduling a time or event to share with the person you have prayed for. As you anticipate this event, make every effort to see from this person's perspective and plan accordingly.

10

Listening as Ears of the Church

At the very end of the Bible stands a mysterious book titled Revelation. Who wrote it? When? Why? And perhaps most importantly, What does it mean? Possible answers to these questions have filled books, dissertations and conferences. They have created a few church and denominational splits, and have spawned heretical groups. Revelation is high drama. Its author is a person named John, "who testifies to everything he saw" (Revelation 1:2). Was this John the now-aging disciple of Jesus who also wrote the Gospel of John and the three letters of John, and the "disciple whom Jesus loved" (John 13:23)? Or was this particular John some unknown later scribe who testified "to everything he saw"?

What John saw unveils some of the most graphic imagery in all of Scripture. At the outset we read that this book is "the revelation from Jesus Christ" (Revelation 1:1). This now risen and ascended Christ, when speaking to John, describes himself as "the Alpha and the Omega . . . who is, and who was, and who is to come, the Almighty" (Revelation 1:8). At the outset we find a series of seven terse letters addressed to seven first-century churches located in what is now western Turkey.

GROUP DISCUSSION. If you were preparing a church evaluation form, what questions would you ask and why?

PERSONAL REFLECTION. Spend time praying for your own church—or the church closest to you. Ask God to reveal any needs there that might benefit from your participation.

Prepare to listen as ears of the church—the church then and the church now. *Read Revelation 1:19–3:21.*

1. Pretend that you are going first-century-church shopping. Which church on this list would you try out first? Why?

2. Which church would be last on your tryout list? Why?

3. Now take a cross-section look at Jesus Christ's message to these seven churches. What does Jesus reveal about himself (see vv. 2:2, 8, 12, 18; 3:1, 7, 14)?

4. What is your impression of Jesus as he describes himself to these churches?

5. Read about the seven churches again. Look for all that Christ values in each church (see vv. 2:2, 6, 9, 13, 19, 24-25; 3:8, 10).

6. Again, read through the letters to these seven churches. Create a list of the criticisms that you find for each church (see vv. 2:4-5, 14-15, 20-23; 3:1-3, 15-17).

7. Place each of the seven church names on slips of paper and place them in a basket. Pair up with one other person and draw one of the church names from the basket. Assume that you are each a leader in this first-century church and that you must help your church through its future as described in the biblical text. Spend about ten minutes talking and making notes about how you might help your church prepare (as a church and as individuals) for the situation ahead. Consider sermons, programs, events, practices, study, prayer, classes, physical help, relationship building and appropriate Scripture teachings. An individual doing this study should focus on one church each day for the next week, doing an internal spiritual examination to see if you are tempted in some ways illustrated in this church.

8. Read through the seven letters one more time. Select one or more of the criticisms that might apply to today's churches. What might a similar kind of wrongdoing look like in a church today?

9. What reason for hope do you find for some of these churches?

---

10. Once again read through this text. This time listen with the ears of your church. What compliments in this text do you think Christ might also apply to your church?

What complaints might also apply to your church?

Pray for Christ's church in whatever spot around the world comes to mind.

Now or Later

Drive or walk through a town of your choice. Pause in front of each church you see and pray for the people there, for their leaders, for their ministries, for their community, for their spiritual and relational well-being and even their correction if needed. Ask God the Holy Spirit to direct your prayer.

Leader's Notes

MY GRACE IS SUFFICIENT FOR YOU. (2 COR 12:9)

Leading a Bible discussion can be an enjoyable and rewarding experience. But it can also be *scary*—especially if you've never done it before. If this is your feeling, you're in good company. When God asked Moses to lead the Israelites out of Egypt, he replied, "O Lord, please send someone else to do it!" (Ex 4:13). It was the same with Solomon, Jeremiah and Timothy, but God helped these people in spite of their weaknesses, and he will help you as well.

You don't need to be an expert on the Bible or a trained teacher to lead a Bible discussion. The idea behind these inductive studies is that the leader guides group members to discover for themselves what the Bible has to say. This method of learning will allow group members to remember much more of what is said than a lecture would.

These studies are designed to be led easily. As a matter of fact, the flow of questions through the passage from observation to interpretation to application is so natural that you may feel that the studies lead themselves. This study guide is also flexible. You can use it with a variety of groups—student, professional, neighborhood or church groups. Each study takes forty-five to sixty minutes in a group setting.

There are some important facts to know about group dynamics and encouraging discussion. The suggestions listed below should enable you to effectively and enjoyably fulfill your role as leader.

Preparing for the Study

1. Ask God to help you understand and apply the passage in your own life. Unless this happens, you will not be prepared to lead others. Pray too for the various members of the group. Ask God to open your hearts to the message of his Word and motivate you to action.

2. Read the introduction to the entire guide to get an overview of the entire book and the issues that will be explored.

3. As you begin each study, read and reread the assigned Bible passage to familiarize yourself with it.

4. This study guide is based on the New International Version of the Bible. It will help you and the group if you use this translation as the basis for your study and discussion.

5. Carefully work through each question in the study. Spend time in meditation and reflection as you consider how to respond.

6. Write your thoughts and responses in the space provided in the study guide. This will help you to express your understanding of the passage clearly.

7. It might help to have a Bible dictionary handy. Use it to look up any unfamiliar words, names or places. (For additional help on how to study a passage, see chapter five of *How to Lead a LifeGuide Bible Study*, InterVarsity Press.)

8. Consider how you can apply the Scripture to your life. Remember that the group will follow your lead in responding to the studies. They will not go any deeper than you do.

9. Once you have finished your own study of the passage, familiarize yourself with the leader's notes for the study you are leading. These are designed to help you in several ways. First, they tell you the purpose the study guide author had in mind when writing the study. Take time to think through how the study questions work together to accomplish that purpose. Second, the notes provide you with additional background information or suggestions on group dynamics for various questions. This information can be useful when people have difficulty understanding or answering a question. Third, the leader's notes can alert you to potential problems you may encounter during the study.

10. If you wish to remind yourself of anything mentioned in the leader's notes, make a note to yourself below that question in the study.

Leading the Study

1. Begin the study on time. Open with prayer, asking God to help the group to understand and apply the passage.

2. Be sure that everyone in your group has a study guide. Encourage the group to prepare beforehand for each discussion by reading the introduction to the guide and by working through the questions in the study.

3. At the beginning of your first time together, explain that these studies are meant to be discussions, not lectures. Encourage the members of the group to participate. However, do not put pressure on those who may be hesitant to speak during the first few sessions. You may want to suggest the following guidelines to your group.

☐ Stick to the topic being discussed.

☐ Your responses should be based on the verses which are the focus of the discussion and not on outside authorities such as commentaries or speakers.

☐ These studies focus on a particular passage of Scripture. Only rarely should you refer to other portions of the Bible. This allows for everyone to participate in in-depth study on equal ground.

☐ Anything said in the group is considered confidential and will not be discussed outside the group unless specific permission is given to do so.

☐ We will listen attentively to each other and provide time for each person present to talk.

☐ We will pray for each other.

4. Have a group member read the introduction at the beginning of the discussion.

5. Every session begins with a group discussion question. The question or activity is meant to be used before the passage is read. The question introduces the theme of the study and encourages group members to begin to open up. Encourage as many members as possible to participate, and be ready to get the discussion going with your own response.

This section is designed to reveal where our thoughts or feelings need to be transformed by Scripture. That is why it is especially important not to read the passage before the discussion question is asked. The passage will tend to color the honest reactions people would otherwise give because they are, of course, supposed to think the way the Bible does.

You may want to supplement the group discussion question with an icebreaker to help people to get comfortable. See the community section of *Small Group Idea Book* for more ideas.

You also might want to use the personal reflection question with your group. Either allow a time of silence for people to respond individually or discuss it together.

6. Have a group member (or members if the passage is long) read aloud the passage to be studied. Then give people several minutes to read the passage again silently so that they can take it all in.

7. Question 1 will generally be an overview question designed to briefly survey the passage. Encourage the group to look at the whole passage, but try to avoid getting sidetracked by questions or issues that will be addressed later in the study.

8. As you ask the questions, keep in mind that they are designed to be used just as they are written. You may simply read them aloud. Or you may prefer to express them in your own words.

There may be times when it is appropriate to deviate from the study guide. For example, a question may have already been answered. If so, move on to the next question. Or someone may raise an important question not covered in the guide. Take time to discuss it, but try to keep the group from going off on tangents.

9. Avoid answering your own questions. If necessary, repeat or rephrase them until they are clearly understood. Or point out something you read in the leader's notes to clarify the context or meaning. An eager group quickly becomes passive and silent if they think the leader will do most of the talking.

10. Don't be afraid of silence. People may need time to think about the question before formulating their answers.

11. Don't be content with just one answer. Ask, "What do the rest of you think?" or "Anything else?" until several people have given answers to the question.

12. Acknowledge all contributions. Try to be affirming whenever possible. Never reject an answer. If it is clearly off-base, ask, "Which verse led you to that conclusion?" or again, "What do the rest of you think?"

13. Don't expect every answer to be addressed to you, even though this will probably happen at first. As group members become more at ease, they will begin to truly interact with each other. This is one sign of healthy discussion.

14. Don't be afraid of controversy. It can be very stimulating. If you don't resolve an issue completely, don't be frustrated. Move on and keep it in mind for later. A subsequent study may solve the problem.

15. Periodically summarize what the group has said about the passage. This helps to draw together the various ideas mentioned and gives continuity to the study. But don't preach.

16. At the end of the Bible discussion you may want to allow group members a time of quiet to work on an idea under "Now or Later." Then discuss what you experienced. Or you may want to encourage group members to work on these ideas between meetings. Give an opportunity during the session for people to talk about what they are learning.

17. Conclude your time together with conversational prayer, adapting the prayer suggestion at the end of the study to your group. Ask for God's help in following through on the commitments you've made.

18. End on time.

Many more suggestions and helps are found in *How to Lead a LifeGuide Bible Study*.

Components of Small Groups

A healthy small group should do more than study the Bible. There are four components to consider as you structure your time together.

Nurture. Small groups help us to grow in our knowledge and love of God. Bible study is the key to making this happen and is the foundation of your small group.

Community. Small groups are a great place to develop deep friendships with other Christians. Allow time for informal interaction before and after each study. Plan activities and games that will help you get to know each other. Spend time having fun together going on a picnic or cooking dinner together.

Worship and prayer. Your study will be enhanced by spending time praising God together in prayer or song. Pray for each other's needs and keep track of how God is answering prayer in your group. Ask God to help you to apply what you are learning in your study.

Outreach. Reaching out to others can be a practical way of applying what you are learning, and it will keep your group from becoming self-focused. Host a series of evangelistic discussions for your friends or neighbors. Clean up the yard of an elderly friend. Serve at a soup kitchen together, or spend a day working on a Habitat house.

Many more suggestions and helps in each of these areas are found in *Small Group Idea Book*. Information on building a small group can be found in *Small Group Leaders' Handbook* and *The Big Book on Small Groups* (both from InterVarsity Press). Reading through one of these books would be worth your time.

Study 1. The God Who Speaks. Genesis 1–3.

Purpose: To recognize the power of God's voice as he connects with all he has created.

Reading. This is a long and graphic text. You will better hear the voice of God throughout if you read the words aloud. It will take about fifteen minutes—time well used. If time constraints suggest spreading this study over two sessions, consider breaking after question 6.

Question 2. A lot of theology grows from these first three chapters of the Bible. God's actions of creation and establishing relationship with the humans that he made; God's ongoing care, commands, response to sin; God's provision for redemption—all appear in these opening chapters of Genesis. Consider phrasing each answer with "God is [character description] because he [action]." Or "God showed that he is [character] when he [action]." Or "I think that God is . . . because he . . ."

Question 3. It's possible to spend the entire time together arguing about what the text means when it uses the term "day" in God's creation order. Some argue that the words "evening" and "morning" insists these are twenty-four-hour days as we know them. Others, however, hold an equally high view of Scripture but understand differently the meaning of the word "day." A wise discussion leader will show respect for both views, admitting that the term "day" can encompass a variety of understandings of time, and not force a crisis of choice between science and Creator God.

Question 5. The "image of God" is a complex concept that has occupied theologians throughout the history of Christian thought. Observations include (but are not limited to):

- The image of God is a limitation. We are mere humans, not identical to God. But it is also an amplification: humans reflect God and should live according to God's character qualities (Irenaeus, AD 130–202).

- God is Trinity. Therefore humans are relational in character and in action (Augustine, AD 354–430).

- God rules. Humans also have moral responsibility over all that God has created (Hebrews 2:5-9).

- God is holy and righteous. When God restores his followers by his grace, we begin to hold these God qualities by our re-creation (John Calvin, 1509–1564).

- Human society can reflect the image of God when people create a society of "existence-in-love" (Emil Brunner, 1889–1966).

- The image of God appears in Christ alone (Karl Barth, 1886–1968).

(These views are summarized from Sinclair B. Ferguson, "Image of God," in *New Dictionary of Theology*, ed. Sinclair B. Ferguson, David F. Wright and J. I. Packer [Downers Grove, IL: InterVarsity Press, 1988], 328-39.)

Use question 5 to begin a spiritually healthy view of self as you reflect on God's creation of humans. On a practical level, those who want to better reflect the image of God will try to model his character and follow his teachings. This can begin by knowing God as he presents himself in Scripture.

Question 7. The major difference in the chapters is focus. In Genesis 1 we see creation of the whole universe. Genesis 2 is, in some ways, a retelling of chapter one, but with a singular focus on the creation of humans. Look for differences in tone, detail, connection with God, accountability and relationships.

Question 9. This question sets the stage for the remainder of the study. Genesis 3 is among the most important chapters about the God-human relationship in all of Scripture—surpassed only by the cross. As you compare and contrast God with his created humans, look for similarities, differences and what this implies about ongoing relationship between humans and God.

Question 10. Sharp eyes will note the startlingly prophetic words to the serpent (Satan) in the second half of verse 15, "he will crush your head, and you will strike his heel." Many theologians see these as prophetically hopeful words (in the midst of the curse) toward Jesus Christ. The death of Jesus on the cross would indeed break the power of Satan's rule in a human being—but not without pain. The bruised heel of the Genesis text foreshadows Christ's suffering. Theologians use the term *protoevangelium*, meaning "the first gospel."

Questions 11-12. Use these final questions to reflect in a joyful and also a sobering way about all you have seen in these first three chapters of Scripture.

Study 2. Listening to the God Who Hears. Genesis 16:1-15; 18:1-33.

Purpose: To apprehend that the God who invites us to listen to him also listens to us.

Question 1. Requiring a slave to produce an heir for her master was not unheard of in the ancient world—or even in our own. The value that God places on Hagar by listening to her and speaking directly to her draws sharp contrast to the way her owners treated her as a barely human material asset.

Questions 2-4. If you are working with a group, suggest that two people read aloud the conversation between Hagar and the angel of the Lord, with a third reader picking up the section of the text not spoken by the other two.

Note: The heavenly being described here as "the angel of the Lord" in verses 7 and 9 is later identified by Hagar in verse 13: "You are the God who sees me." Theologian Derek Kidner comments, "A study of 'the Angel of the Lord' passages . . . leaves no room for doubt that the term denotes God Himself as seen in human form; what should be added is that 'Angel', by its meaning 'messenger', implies that God, made visible, is at the same time God *sent*. . . . the pre-existent Son" (Derek Kidner, *Genesis*, Tyndale Old Testament Commentaries [Downers Grove, IL: IVP Academic, 2008], 36).

Question 7. "The Lord" of Genesis 18:17 and following is no doubt the same being who previously spoke with Hagar. Kidner compares "the Lord's" conversation with Abraham to John 15:15, where Jesus, speaking to his disciples, says, "I no longer call you servants, because a servant does not know his master's business. Instead, I have called you friends" (ibid., 132). John Calvin spoke earlier in a similar vein as he comments on the opening of Genesis 19: "why [has] one of the three angels . . . disappeared, and two only are come to Sodom? . . . [I]t was granted to Abraham, as a peculiar favour, that God would not only send him two messengers from the angelic host, but that, in a more familiar manner, he would manifest himself to him in his own Son" (John Calvin, *Commentaries on the First Book of Moses, Called Genesis* [Grand Rapids: Baker Books, 2005], 495).

Question 9. "Richer man," of course, implies more than a money-gold-silver-land kind of wealth, though Abraham seems to have benefited from these as well. Consider his riches in the broadest sense possible.

Note: Genesis 17 signals one the most important events in Old Testament history. In it, God calls Abraham (Hagar's owner) to be father of God's own chosen people, announces that Abraham and Sarah (his real wife) would father a child (Isaac) in their old age, and that from this child would come "twelve rulers" who would make a great nation—the Jews with their twelve tribes. God also commanded Abraham to begin the rite of circumcision of all males in his household, including Ishmael. Abraham obeyed. Then, before any of the promises come to pass, Abraham also has a personal encounter with God.

Study 3. Listening to the God of Covenant. Exodus 33:7–34:14.

Purpose: To draw strength from our covenant relationship with God.

Question 2. Notice throughout that Moses serves as intercessor between God and the people God has called him to lead. Why did Joshua remain near the tent of meeting? The young Joshua would become the next leader of God's people. Perhaps he too had unrecorded up-close God encounters in this place. Or perhaps his duty was to guard that place.

Question 3. Much of the impact of this text comes from the covenant relationship between Moses and God as established in their conversation. Reading aloud (in dialogue if possible) will help the text come alive.

Questions 4–5. Make a careful list drawn from Exodus 33:13-14, 17, 19-20; 34:1-3, 9, 10-14. Working with these covenant requirements can look tedious if they become simply two lists of tasks. Pause every now and then to think through the tasks to consider how they established relationships between Moses, the people and God.

Question 6. Why would God, who in verse 11 "would speak to Moses face to face, as a man speaks with his friend," by verses 20-23 have Moses tucked into a rock crevice because "no one may see me and live"? James Hoffmeier suggests,

> It seems then that Moses desires to know more of God's character and person than he has experienced to this point. God will only partially fulfill Moses' request; he will let his goodness pass before him (v. 9) for no man can see God's face and live. . . . Something of God's eternal qualities are revealed to Moses. But even in this manifestation Moses has to be protected (vv. 21-22). God's glory is to be more fully revealed

in Jesus Christ. (James Hoffmeier, "Exodus," *Evangelical Commentary on the Bible,* ed. Walter Elwell [Grand Rapids: Baker Books, 1989], 61)

We might notice that for Moses, God's protection is highly personal. God covers Moses (now surrounded by rock) with his own hand as God reveals to his servant what he is able to absorb without harm.

Question 6. Use this question to think personally and together about your relationship with God. This may suggest areas where you can encourage spiritual development in one another (if in a group) or better nurture your own relationship with the God who loves you and calls you (through covenant) as his own.

Question 8. Each appearance of the word "name" has varying meaning and significance as it helps define who Moses is, who God is and the relationship between them.

Question 10. Discuss the connections and limitations of this rather strange event. It seems that God allows his people to know him—but not completely. In C. S. Lewis's Narnia books he writes of the great and powerful lion Aslan as a Christ figure. But he cautions the children to always remember "Aslan is not a tame lion." Lewis likely drew that insight about God's nature from these and similar biblical texts. God invites us to approach him carefully. There is much that we do not and cannot know about God.

Question 12. We think of the term "jealous" as a bad or even evil quality. Yet God, who is rightly sovereign over all things, demands that we recognize him as such. The future of God's covenant people would have them surrounded over and over by other gods. They were not even to enter into a treaty with the occupants of the land God would return to them, because a treaty might include recognition or worship of these false gods. In a society full of multiple gods, monotheism would be a challenge, a constant threat to people following the one true and only God.

Study 4. Listening to God When All Is Lost. 1 Kings 19:1-21; 2 Kings 2:1-13.

Purpose: To value God's presence, particularly in times of discouragement.

Question 1. Elijah faced a death warrant from Queen Jezebel. But he also faced serious hardship (perhaps death) from heat and lack of food and water in the desert. In addition, his mental and spiritual torment led him to even desire or prefer death over continued existence under these circumstances.

Question 4. Pause here in your focus on the text to think together about your own times of experiencing a need beyond your own resources. Perhaps you also have experienced God's presence and help during that time. Or perhaps your experience was only of haunting longing. It is helpful to remember that God is present with his people even when unseen and unnoticed. It's appropriate to express both thanks and longing at those times—even as we view them in hindsight.

Question 6. The mighty forces of nature as shown in wind, earthquake and fire (Elijah knowing that God ruled all of these) cascading into God's "gentle whisper" of verse 12 speaks volumes about God's authority and power in contrast with his gentleness and compassion toward Elijah. To be loved and protected by such a strong God must have reassured this beleaguered prophet.

Question 9. Elisha's physical strength to manage twelve yokes of oxen and his quick response to Elijah's request reveal a man ready and able to work for God. The fact that he slaughtered his oxen, burned his farm equipment and cooked a supply of food showed that he was willing to burn his bridges behind him. Some readers wonder about Elijah's rather strange answer to Elisha's request to kiss his parents goodbye. The best explanation seems that Elijah intends to turn authority about these and other matters over to Elisha—along with his cloak. "What have I done to you?" might be rendered "I've put you in charge. Do as you like, under God's provision."

Question 11. The transfer of Elijah's cloak forms an interesting symbol. It suggests the travel life of a prophet who would need portable covering. It also suggests authority. When Elijah used the cloak to part the Jordan River in 2 Kings 2:7-8, he echoed the similar authority that Moses used as he stretched out his hand to part the Red Sea, enabling the Hebrews to escape Egypt (Exodus 14:21). Elijah's act also echoes the parting of the Jordan River when Joshua led them into the Promised Land (Joshua 3:14-17). Each of these signaled a new era under a new leader for God's chosen people.

Study 5. Listening as Worship. Ecclesiastes 5:1-7.

Purpose: To broaden our practice of worship so that we worship not only with mind and voice but also with ears and heart.

Question 1. You will find ten or twelve direct commands in this text. List them, making written notes if helpful.

Question 2. The text doesn't give a list of reasons for these worship commands, but you will find hints there. Like much of Scripture, these hints point toward God's character, his nature, his being. Already we see that worship is not like paying a bill for services rendered but recognition of God himself as worthy of worship from his created beings regardless of their circumstances.

Question 6. Do we make vows during worship? If your church uses a bulletin or order of worship, try reading through the words of the songs, Scriptures, readings, responses and prayers. What did you promise God in church last week? If you do not use a church bulletin, during your next worship service take a note every time you say, sing, pray or read a promise to God. Use these notes to remind yourself that worship is not just something we sit through but something we do. Part of our task of listening to God is listening to what we ourselves say to God during worship. We can expect that our attentive God will receive these promises and hold us to them.

Question 7. The words of verse 6, "Do not let your mouth lead you into sin," cautions all of us. Examples of "mouth sins" appear in the text before and after the statement. Here the wisdom writer is speaking specifically of promises made to God and about God. Sometimes instead of talking we should stand in awe of God. This awe might inspire us toward silence. Afterward, our actions can grow out of thoughtful consideration of God's character. Michael Eaton says of verse seven's warning, "The *dreaming* (7) must mean something like day-dreaming, casualness, unreality in approaching God. This and the flood of careless words in prayer are both marks of the *meaningless* (frustrated, awry) world. Fear of God is the remedy" (Michael A. Eaton, "Ecclesiastes," in *New Bible Commentary* [Downers Grove, IL: IVP Academic, 1994], 115-16).

Question 8. Michael Eaton cautions, "people are prone to carry their illusions with them while they worship and also to talk without thinking. If a vow is made this way, the worshipper is treading on dangerous ground. The remedy is to *fear God*" (Michael A. Eaton, *Ecclesiastes*, Tyndale Old Testament Commentaries [Downers Grove, IL: IVP Academic, 2009], 115-16).

Question 10. This worship text from an ancient wisdom writer offers caution and council for us today. Pull out one sentence or phrase that you find helpful, interesting, inspiring or an aid to your worship. If you are with a group, share with others why this phrase held your attention.

Study 6. Responsibility of a God Listener. Ezekiel 33.

Purpose: To appreciate and participate in the responsibilities of a God listener.

Question 2. Use this question to survey information found in the text. Responsibilities of a watchman appear in verses 3, 6, 7-8, 10-11 and 25-28. For protections, see verses 4-5 and 9. John B. Taylor says, "Everything was subordinated to his almost overwhelming sense of obligation and responsibility. He was a watchman, and if he failed to warn the people, their blood would be upon him" (John B. Taylor, *Ezekiel*, Tyndale Old Testament Commentaries [Downers Grove, IL: IVP Academic, 2009], 31).

Question 6. In verse 22 we read that God opened Ezekiel's mouth and he was no longer silent. Ezekiel's mouth (ability to speak) comes up at several places in this book. In Ezekiel 3:26-27 we read that God will exercise control over Ezekiel's mouth. "But when I speak to you, I will open your mouth and you shall say to them, 'This is what the Sovereign LORD says.'" In Ezekiel 24:15-27, when Ezekiel's wife dies, God orders Ezekiel not to mourn in the usual vocal way but that later "a fugitive will come to tell you the news. At that time your mouth will be opened; you will speak with him and will no longer be silent" (vv. 26-27). So in Ezekiel 33:22 we read that God opened Ezekiel's mouth and "I was no longer silent." Did Ezekiel remain without speech throughout much of his life? Probably not, but clearly the book highlights that Ezekiel's speech is God guided with its frequent "The word of the Lord came to me." And Ezekiel's voice was also sometimes restrained by God.

Question 7. Just as in the Old Testament God called a people to be his own, the New Testament also speaks of God's people as a group. As a part of his church throughout the world, we too belong to this body of believers. The watchmen in ancient texts had both military and spiritual callings. Military watchmen stood on the city wall and watched for enemies who might approach. Watchmen also watched the city gates, noting who came in and out. Watchmen were protectors of the people. They alerted their people to danger before attackers arrived. The prophet Ezekiel spoke of himself as a spiritual watchman. He warned his people of their spiritual danger before they fell into serious separation from God. Sometimes his people heeded his warnings, sometimes not.

Many Christians today also experience the care of a spiritual watcher or provider. Sometimes there is mutual accountability where two or more people nurture each other's faith, encourage each other as Christ followers or warn about spiritual hazards ahead. This happens within families, friendships, churches, or even formal mentor relationships. Most Christians have benefited from this kind of care at one time or another, sometimes even though they were not aware of some watcher-like care at the time. Ezekiel's example as a God-appointed spiritual watchman can help us reflect on when and by whom we have received that kind of care, and perhaps also when we might be responsible to give it.

Study 7. Listening to Understand. Luke 24:13-53.

Purpose: To listen through the ears of Jesus' disciples as they learn the meaning of his death, burial, resurrection and ascension.

Question 1. The disciples had not expected Jesus to die, though he had prepared them as well as possible for this reality. Much less, they didn't expect his resurrection or even believe it at first. They could hardly have been more startled to find him walking beside them on their seven-mile walk to Emmaus. We must remember that transportation for common folk (as were the disciples) consisted of their sandaled feet. Seven miles would provide between two and three hours for conversation. We can read aloud the words of this text, so full of meaning, in about seven minutes. Yet we long to ask them what more they discussed on that trip. That walk and talk prepared them for Pentecost some forty days distant, and for a life (and death) of mission carrying the words of Jesus throughout the then-known world. No doubt their shock and grief at having observed his grizzly death and now the joy of renewed conversation must have made them nearly wild with questions (and the most avid listeners on earth).

Question 3. Search the text looking for spots where you would have felt enlightened or would have wanted to interrupt their conversation and ask a question.

Question 4. Feel free to draw on two thousand years of Christian insight to imagine what these two understood when "their eyes were opened."

Question 5-6. Use these questions to put yourself in the sandals of those two disciples who were privileged with the Emmaus Road experience. You are now speaking with other disciples that you presume were similarly close to Jesus. You don't understand or hardly believe some of what you heard from Jesus. What would you say? Not say? What picture would you want to paint for their benefit or your own? Notice particularly the significance of verses 30 and 35.

Question 7. We read in verse 45 that Jesus opened their minds so that they could understand the Scriptures. This might be something like a full doctoral program in Bible and theology, a full reading of a substantial theological library and the ability to grasp it all in a moment—with Jesus as teacher. We might notice that among those people present for this Christ-revealed understanding of Bible and theology were the future writers of ten books that would become the New Testament.

Question 8. It's hard to find a single phrase of this text that is not important. Review the text line by line looking for its significance. For example, why was Jesus' first word "Peace"? What is the significance that they thought he was a ghost? (They knew he was dead; they'd seen him die.) Why did he ask about their doubts? (Any sane person would doubt that Jesus was alive after crucifixion and burial.) What would you have learned if you had been able to touch him? What would you have gained by watching him swallow food?

Question 9. This question switches from the understanding granted in verse 45 to the visual scenes of this event. Work through verses 30-53 again, this time looking for visual impact at each point and what you would have seen by being there.

Question 10. These final hours with Jesus were not an experience that could be ignored. No one present could return to normal life. The commission of verses 46-50 would not allow them to remain at home for long. The "power from on high" described in verse 49 would forever set them apart from other people. They would have the responsibility of composing much of the New Testament, including three biographical books about the life of Christ. They would be blessed with power of the Holy Spirit (see Acts 2). Most would die as martyrs. The Christian faith would spring from their testimony and spread throughout the world. Eternal life (or death) of all future generations rested on their mission. They had to get it right.

Study 8. Holy Help in Listening. John 14:5-31.

Purpose: To better understand God as Trinity and so to particularly value God the Holy Spirit.

Question 1. Note that this section of Scripture is part of Jesus' final conversation with his disciples. He had already washed their feet at their final meal together and they were probably walking toward Gethsemane. The questions appear in verse 5, 8 and 22. After you have read the entire text, try paraphrasing and elaborating on each question in the tone of voice you think likely came from the person asking that question.

Question 2. This time try paraphrasing how Jesus responded to Thomas with the tone of voice you think Jesus might have used. In Jesus' day the Roman and Greek society he lived within believed in many gods for many purposes. The concept of "one way to one God" would have offended and angered those who were used to appeasing multiple deities. Today's culture holds similar tension. We often hear, "There are many ways to God." The Jewish faith holds that there is only one God. In this text Jesus claims that he is "the way, the truth and the life" and that "no one comes to the Father except through me." Then he goes on to explain God as Trinity (three persons composing one God). With these statements he offended most in his own culture and many in ours.

Questions 4-5. All of us would respond differently if wearing Philip's sandals. Encouragements might include three years of experience in Christ's presence (v. 9); his claim to oneness with the Father, that they are "in" one another (vv. 9-10); that the Father even speaks through Jesus, so they have already heard words from the Father (v. 10). If they couldn't get their heads around that oneness, then consider the miracles. They made no human sense either. Yet the disciples saw these miracles with their own eyes (v. 11). Jesus promised them a special power from God through the Holy Spirit, who would come to the disciples "because I am going to the Father" (v. 12). Jesus also offers them the gift and power of prayer (v. 14).

Question 6. Judas seemed to grasp that Jesus left a huge task in their laps. We can imagine the Christ-follower Judas complained something to the effect of, "You are leaving us holding the bag! What if we mess up? Who is going to believe in an absent Jesus? All they know is that you died! This job is way bigger than we are." (Notice that this is not Judas Iscariot, the one who betrayed the Lord.)

Question 7. Find encouragement and reassurance in almost every phrase of verses 23-31.

Question 8. Linger on this question so the reassurance of Jesus becomes your own, not just a first-century story.

Question 9. The concept of God as Trinity appears many places in Scripture, but here it is outlined quite fully by Christ. You can find some fifteen to twenty bits of information about God as Trinity in verses 7-31. These include but are not limited to: if you know Jesus, you also know God the Father (v. 7); if you have seen Jesus, you have seen the Father (v. 9); Jesus is in the Father, and the Father is in Jesus (v. 10); the words of Jesus are also the words of the Father (v. 10); miracles testify to Christ's deity (v. 11); we can pray to God in Jesus' name (v. 13); the Advocate (Spirit) will be present in the absence of Jesus (v. 16); this Spirit will be both in and with the disciples (v. 17); love toward Jesus brings returning love from the Father (v. 21) resulting in a circle of love given and received (vv. 21-23); words from Jesus are also words from the Father (v. 26). Note further explanation and reassurance in verses 28-31.

Question 10. Gauge the pace of your study to allow a time of silent meditation on this question. Then, if you are in a group, respond to one another as you share your thoughts.

Study 9. Listening as Self-Discipline. James 1:19-27.

Purpose: To deliberately work at becoming better listeners to God and to one another.

Question 1. Read this question before reading the text. This will allow you to mentally put yourself into the setting of those who first received this letter.

Questions 2-3. Some of us are natural listeners; others are not. But even those who enjoy listening can better listen with purpose because of this text. Listening is not passive. It requires physical and mental effort. Hearing, on the other hand, can be passive. We hear background noise. To listen well we must mentally close out distractions, drop what we are doing, pay attention to gestures and voice inflections to discern intensity of meaning, ask questions of clarification, probe for a deeper meaning, discipline ourselves not to interrupt or turn the conversation toward our own interests. When merely hearing, we can perceive background noise and mentally dismiss it as unimportant. We can do the same with a person. The discipline of listening requires attention and a measure of self-denial, of putting aside (at least for the moment) other sounds and thoughts. James sees listening as work: the work of listening to God through Scripture; the work of listening to another at the cost or discipline of dropping other interests for those moments.

Question 4. Make a mental or written list of the dos and don'ts in these verses. You'll notice that by verses 20-21 James shifts his attention from listening as a general people skill to the more specific discipline of preparing our minds and souls to better listen to God.

Question 5. James uses the illustration of a mirror to show what God's Word can become. An untidy person can take a quick look in the mirror, make a minor adjustment and continue the day with no further thought about grooming. Many of us are tempted to treat God's Word in similar fashion. We give our souls a ten-minute cleanup by reading, praying or thinking on God's Word. Then we turn our thoughts to other matters, and never give God's instructions a second thought throughout our day. Our relationship to the mirror is kiss-and-run. James warns against taking God's Word, values, standards and teachings with this kind of inattention. In doing so, we deceive ourselves by thinking we are more spiritual than we are.

Questions 6-7. If you are meeting with a church-going group, consider asking ahead of time that each participant bring a copy of the most recent church bulletin from his or her church. Bring a few extra copies of your own to share. Use this question to find practical ways to continue prayer, meditation, study or life correction as guided by something said, read, prayed or sung during a worship service. Some Christians make this a regular Monday-morning spiritual discipline as they review their most recent service of worship, focusing on one small section to think and pray for its continued impact in their lives.

Question 8. James seems to enjoy startling his readers with yet higher demands. As if the ongoing moral mirror of self-examination in verse 23 were not enough, James now adds discipline of our speech to the duty list. For most of us, speech is as natural as breathing. Yet James instructs us to curb our tongues and instead go to work on behalf of those who are needy and vulnerable. Who are the "orphans and widows" of your own community? The homeless? The mentally ill? Single parents? The undereducated? Before we scurry off to pick up this challenge, James gives us one practical caution:

keep to the moral high road so as not to become "polluted by the world" we are attempting to rescue.

Question 9. Consider ways in this study you have already defined as good listening. This time think how these practices might help you better walk beside the "widows and orphans" in your setting.

Question 10. Focus on one or more of your current relationships that might benefit by this kind of other-focused listening.

Study 10. Listening as Ears of the Church. Revelation 1:19–3:21.

Purpose: To understand what is important to Christ about his churches.

Note: Working through this study can take more than the usual small-group meeting time. If you feel time crunched, consider breaking for a second study beginning at question 7. You can open the second study with a brief review of the first.

Questions 1-2. If some in your group are not familiar with this book, invite them to read Revelation 1:1-3 with you. After this introduction it will be helpful to a group if you read the first two questions to them before the remaining text is read. With all of the dramatic events recorded so graphically in the book of Revelation, a bit of theater in the reading will help listeners get into the scene.

Question 3. Christ's message to each of the seven churches follows a similar outline. Most start with Jesus identifying and describing himself. You'll find information about his nature and identity in the verses supplied. In the message to the church in Philadelphia we read that the speaker (Jesus) "holds the key of David." Theologian Leon Morris writes, "probably it is admission to the city of David, the heavenly Jerusalem . . . and this Christ alone gives or withholds" (Leon Morris, *Revelation*, Tyndale New Testament Commentaries [Downers Grove, IL: IVP Academic, 2009], 81).

Question 5. In some ways these chapters read like a report card on seven churches. You'll find good points about Ephesus in 2:2, 6; Smyrna in 2:9; Pergamum in 2:13, 19; Thyatira in 2:24-25; nothing for Sardis; Philadelphia in 3:8, 10; and nothing for Laodicea.

Question 6. Criticisms appear as follows: Ephesus in 2:4-5; Smyrna has no criticism; Pergamum in 2:14-15; Thyatira in 2:20-23; Sardis in 3:1-3; Philadelphia is not criticized; Laodicea is warned in 3:15-17. Use this opportunity not only to list the sins or errors mentioned but also why those sins might be tempting, what they might look like in practice and how they are harmful to the church. If your time is limited, consider closing the study at this point and begin a second session at question 7.

Question 7. Prepare ahead of time small pieces of paper listing each church. Ask that each pair come up with three or four recommendations for their particular church. If time allows (and your group is small) draw again so that all seven churches are covered.

Question 9. Several times now you have gone through the seven churches looking for some particular interest. This time, look for hope. Then draw on that hope as you consider your own fears and troubles.

Questions 10. "All Scripture is God-breathed and is useful for teaching, rebuking, correcting and training in righteousness" (2 Timothy 3:16). Use the admonition given to the seven churches to spot similar conditions (the good and not so good) in the church you are most familiar with. Perhaps this exercise will lead you toward correcting any weaknesses and to find joy in your church's God-enabled strengths.

Carolyn Nystrom is a career writer with some eighty titles to her name. She also serves as stated clerk of Rivers and Lakes Presbytery, a four-state body of churches in the Evangelical Presbyterian Church.